Rhinoceros

by Grace Hansen

Abdo
AFRICAN ANIMALS
Kids

abdopublishing.com

Published by Abdo Kids, a division of ABDO, P.O. Box 398166, Minneapolis, Minnesota 55439.

Printed in China

102017

012018

THIS BOOK CONTAINS RECYCLED MATERIALS

Photo Credits: Alamy, iStock, Shutterstock

Production Contributors: Teddy Borth, Jennie Forsberg, Grace Hansen

Design Contributors: Dorothy Toth, Laura Mitchell

Publisher's Cataloging in Publication Data

Names: Hansen, Grace, author.

Title: Rhinoceros / by Grace Hansen.

Description: Minneapolis, Minnesota : Abdo Kids, 2018. | Series: African animals | Includes glossary, index and online resource (page 24).

Identifiers: LCCN 2017943137 | ISBN 9781532104213 (lib.bdg.) | ISBN 9781532105333 (ebook) | ISBN 9781532105890 (Read-to-me ebook)

Subjects: LCSH: Rhinoceroses--Juvenile literature. | Zoology--Africa--Juvenile literature.

Classification: DDC 599.66 --dc23

LC record available at https://lccn.loc.gov/2017943137

Table of Contents

Rhino Habitat

Rhinoceroses live in Africa.

They are found in **grasslands**.

Black rhinos mainly live in eastern Africa. They spend most of their days near watering holes. They stay cool by **lounging** in the shade.

Body

Black rhinos are actually gray. But they roll in mud to protect their skin. This makes them look darker than they are.

Black rhinos weigh between 1,700 and 3,000 pounds (771.1 and 1,360.8 kg)! They are 4.5 to 5.5 feet (1.4 to 1.7 m) tall. They are between 10 and 13 feet (3 to 4 m) long.

Black rhinos have two horns. The front horn is longer than the back one. Rhinos use their horns for protection.

Food

Rhinos enjoy **lazy** days. They are much more active at night. They search for their favorite plants to eat.

A black rhino uses its upper lip to grasp and pull leaves from plants. Sometimes it will eat the entire plant, not just the leaves!

Baby Rhinos

Female rhinos usually have one baby at a time. Baby rhinos weigh between 55 and 100 pounds (24.9 and 45.4 kg).

Baby rhinos drink their mothers' milk for about 18 months. At two weeks old, baby rhinos eat leaves too. Babies stay with their mothers for 2 to 3 years.

More Facts

- Rhinos spend most of their lives alone. But females still make very good mothers. They are very protective of their babies.
- Rhinos can live for 30 to 50 years in the wild.
- A rhino's horn can regrow if it is broken off.

Glossary

grassland – a large area of land covered by grass.

lazy – not willing to give much effort.

lounging – to lie down or sit in a very relaxed way.

Index